Mel Bay Presents Stefan Grossman's Guitar Workshop Audio Series

Beginner's Blues Guitar

By Fred Sokolow

Contents

> **Fred Sokolow has other instructional books, tapes, videos & CDs. For a free catalog, write to:**
>
> **Sokolow Music**
> **P.O. Box 491264**
> **Los Angeles CA 90049**

1 2 3 4 5 6 7 8 9 0

Visit us on the Web at http://www.melbay.com – E-mail us at email@melbay.com

CD #1 – Blues Accompaniment in E

#2* : TUNING THE GUITAR

E (1st)
B (2nd)
G (3rd)
D (4th)
A (5th)
E (6th)

#3 : CHORDS FOR THE KEY of E

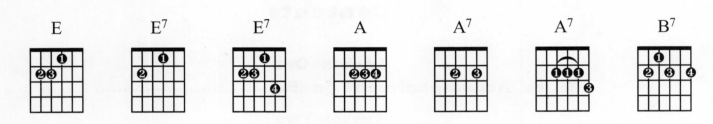

#4 : EARLY MORNING BLUES (Slow Blues)

E7 / / / A7 / / / E7 / / / / / /
Up early in the morning, blues fallin' down like rain.

A7 / / / / / A7 / / / E7 / / / / / /
Up early in the morning, blues fallin' down like rain.

B7 / / / A7 / / / E / A / E / B7 /
Deep down in my heart I felt an achin' pain.

E7 / / / A7 / / / E7 / / / / / /
Ain't it hard to wake up, wake up all by yourself.

A7 / / / / / / E7 / / / / / /
Ain't it hard to wake up, wake up all by yourself.   *When the*

B7 / / / A7 / / / E7 / A7 / E / B7 /
One you're lovin' has gone off with someone else.

On EARLY MORNING BLUES:
Brush down with thumb on each chord or slash, or…
Brush down twice with the thumb on each chord or slash, for a "ba-bump, ba-bump" rhythm.

* These numbers refer to the track numbers and elapsed time (where relevant) on the CD.

#6 : AIRPORT BLUES

E   / / /   E7 / / /   A7   /   /   /   / / / /

Take me to the airport, won't you put me on a plane;   *this*

E   /   /   /   B7   /   /   /   E / A7 / E B7 / /

Smoggy old city, said it's drivin' me insane.

E   /   /   /   / / / /   A7   /   /   /   /   /   /

Goin' down, downtown now, tell me don't you wanna go ?   *I'm gonna*

E   /   /   /   /   B7   /   /   /   E7   / A7 / E B7 / /

Hit the ground runnin' 'cause walkin' is much too slow.

On AIRPORT BLUES:
For every chord or slash, brush down with the thumb and up with the finger, for a "bump-ba-bump-ba" rhythm.

#7, 0:50 : TURNAROUND

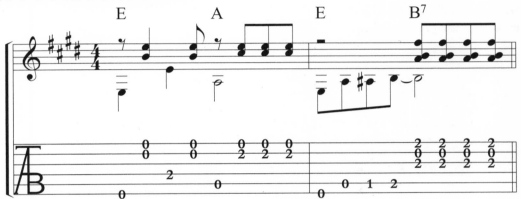

#8 : BOOGIE BASS
for THAT'S ALRIGHT and AIRPORT BLUES

#9 : BOOGIE BASS
for THAT'S ALRIGHT

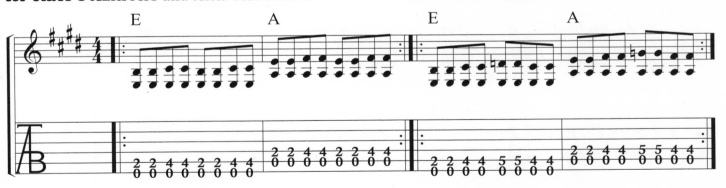

#9 : THAT'S ALRIGHT

E7   A7   E7

That's alright, that's alright with me.

A7   E7

That's alright, that's alright with me.

B7   A7   E7

Anyway you want it, that's the way it's gonna be.

3

#10 : BOOGIE BASS
(also used on EARLY MORNING BLUES)

#11 : EARLY MORNING BLUES
(more verses, with boogie bass lines)

E7   A7   E7
I wonder when, I wonder when my baby's comin' home.

             A7   E7
I wonder when, I wonder when, I wonder when my baby's comin' home.

             B7   A7   E7
You know it seems like such a long, long time since my baby's been gone.

E7   A7   E7
In the evening, can't you hear me when I call.

             A7   E7
In the evening, can't you hear me when I call.

B7   A7   E7
Late in the night time, that's when I miss you most of all.

#12 : BOOGIE BASS for TWELVE BAR BLUES

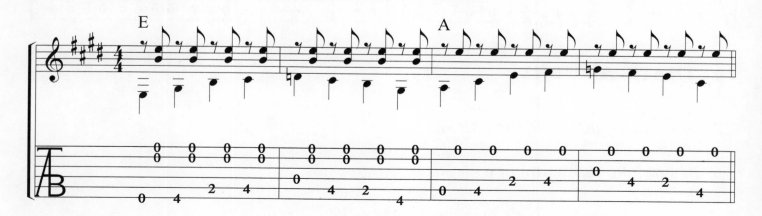

#12 : TWELVE BAR BLUES

E7   A7   E7
Twelve bar blues, twelve bar blues, twelve bar blues, twelve bar blues,

B7   A7   E7
Twelve bar blues, you can play it all night and day.

#12, 1:15 : TWELVE BAR BLUES

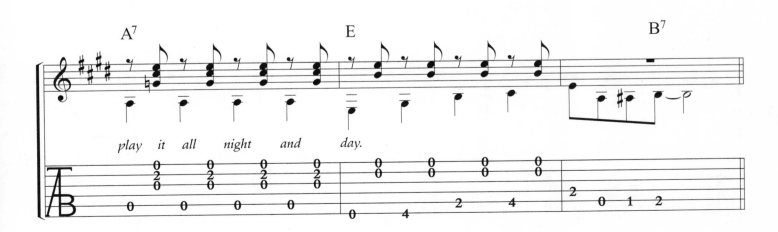

5

#15 : MOVEABLE CHORDS

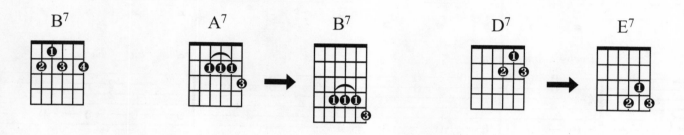

#16 : EARLY MORNING BLUES

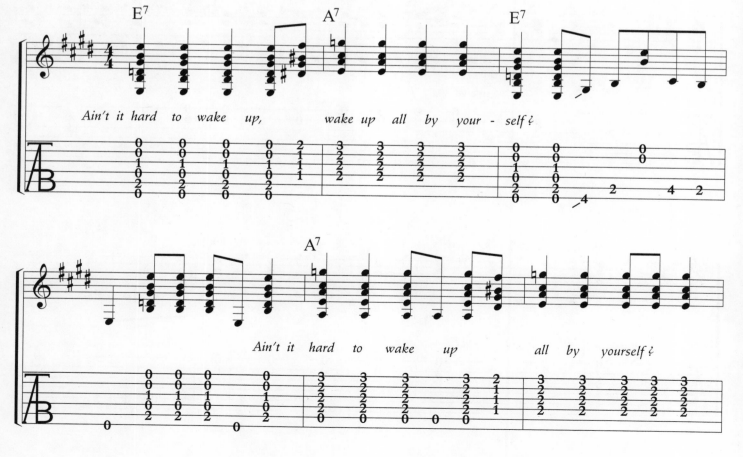

Ain't it hard to wake up, wake up all by your - self?

Ain't it hard to wake up all by yourself?

#18, 1:12

7

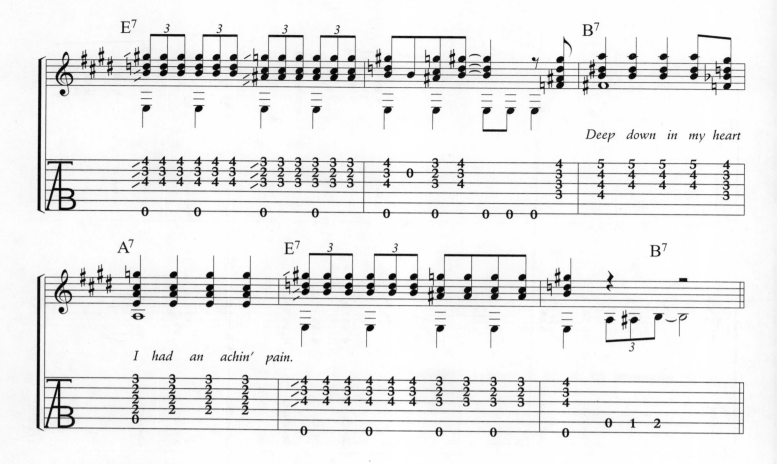

Deep down in my heart

I had an achin' pain.

TURNAROUNDS
#18, 5:00

#18, 5:25

19 : THAT'S ALRIGHT

That's alright,   that's alright with me.

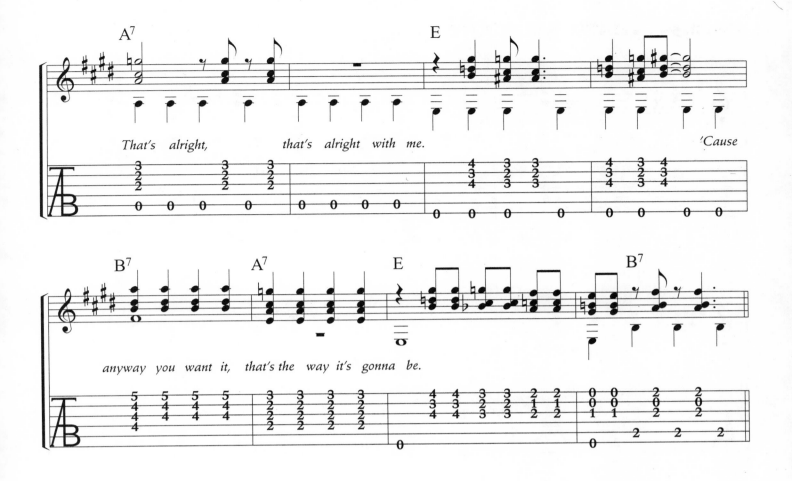

That's alright,   that's alright with me.   'Cause

anyway you want it, that's the way it's gonna be.

#19, 1:35 : EARLY MORNING BLUES
(additional verse)

(D7 up 2 frets)   (up 1 fret)   (up 2 frets)
I believe,   *I believe I'll go back home.*

    A7   (D7 up 2)
I believe,   *I believe I'll go back home.*

    (A7 up 2 frets)   A7   E7
You know I get this funny feeling, I've been gone too long.

#20 : NOTES for FILLS

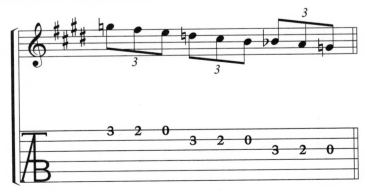

9

#20, 2:39 : THAT'S ALL RIGHT

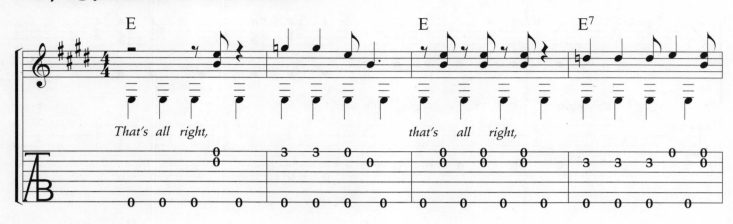

That's all right,   that's all right,

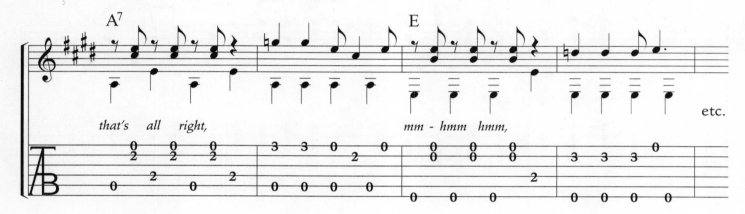

that's all right,   mm - hmm hmm,   etc.

#21, 0:53 : AIRPORT BLUES

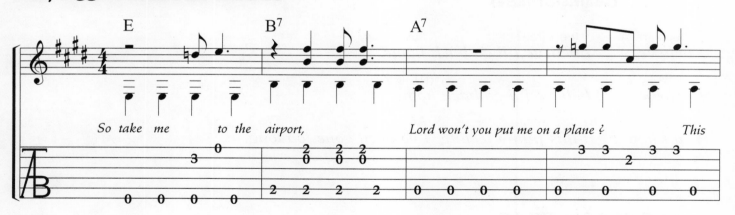

So take me   to the airport,   Lord won't you put me on a plane ¿   This

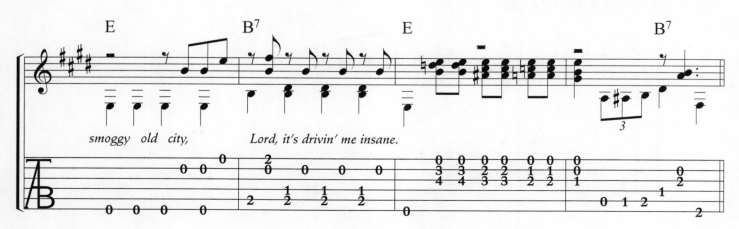

smoggy old city,   Lord, it's drivin' me insane.

10

#21, 2:30 : TWELVE BAR BLUES

#22, 0:50 : ANOTHER TURNAROUND FILL

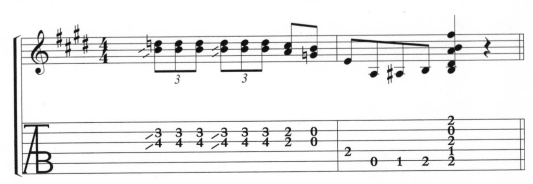

#22, 2:40 : THAT'S ALL RIGHT

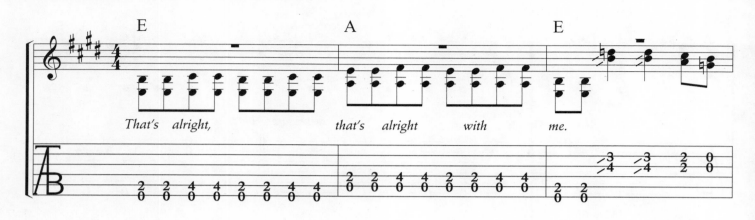

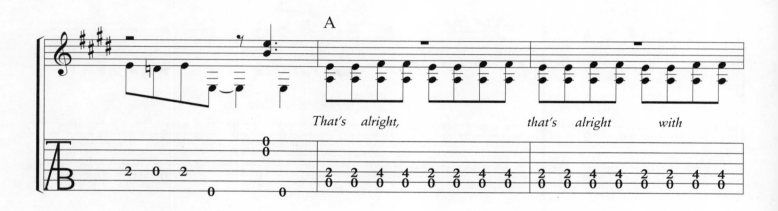

#22, 3:48 : TWELVE BAR BLUES

Same old thing,

same old thing,

etc.

CD #2 – Blues Accompaniment in C and G

#3 : CHORDS FOR THE KEY of C

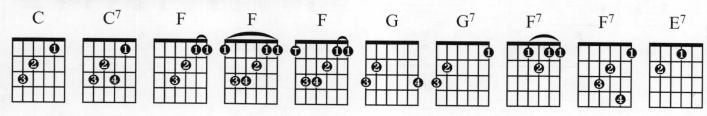

#4 : BASIC FINGERPICKING PATTERNS

#4 : HESITATION BLUES

C
I got hesitatin' feet, hesitatin' shoes.

                                     C7
Angels up in heaven sing the hesitation blues. Tell me

F   C   G7   C
How long must I wait ¿ Can I get you now, or must I hesitate ¿

C
Standin' on the corner with a dollar in my hand,

                                C7
I'm lookin' for a woman who's lookin' for a man. Tell me…(etc.)

C
The eagle on a dollar says "In God we trust."

                                     C7
A woman says she wants a man but wants to see a dollar first. Tell me…(etc.)

C
If the river was whiskey and I was a duck,

                              C7
I'd swim to the bottom and never come up. Tell me…(etc.)

#5 : PATTERNS WITH ALTERNATING BASS

#6 : BASS RUNS

Repeat each 2-bar phrase over and over

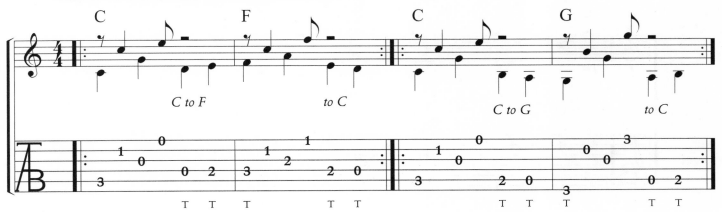

C to F   *to C*   *C to G*   *to C*

#6, 1:41

Doo doo doo...etc.   *Tell me how long*

do I have to wait?   *Can I*

15

get you now,   or must I hesitate ¿

#7 : TURNAROUND

C to G   to C

#8 : COCAINE

C   C7
Cocaine's for horses, not for men.

F
Doctor says it'd kill me but he didn't say when.

C   F   G7   C
Cocaine, run all 'round my brain.

     E7
Come here mama, come here quick, this old cocaine's makin' me sick.   F

C   F   G7   C
Cocaine, run all 'round my brain.

C   C7
Walkin' down Twelfth Street, turned up Main,

F
Lookin' for the man who sells cocaine (etc.)

#9, 0:30 : AIRPORT BLUES

Take me   to the airport,   won't you   put   me   on   a   plane ?

etc.

#9 : AIRPORT BLUES

C   E7   F
Take me to the airport, won't you put me on a plane,

        C   G7   C   C7   F   C   G7
This smoggy old city, it's drivin' me insane.

C   E7   F
I'm goin' down, downtown now, tell me don't you wanna go ?

       C   G7   C   C7   F   C   G7
I'm gonna hit the ground runnin' 'cause walkin' is much too slow.

In the next tune, use this F minor chord for the turnaround:

C   C7   F   Fm   C   G7

Fm

#9, 3:40 : AIRPORT BLUES

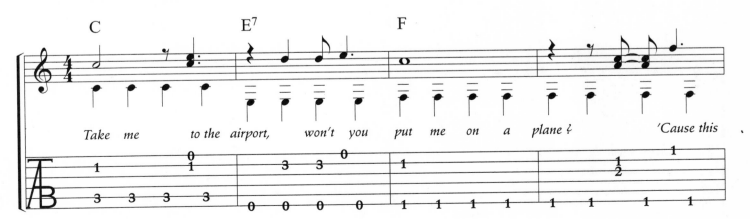

Take me   to the airport,   won't you   put   me   on   a   plane ?   'Cause this

17

smoggy old city drivin' me insane.

#10 : EARLY MORNING BLUES

Up early in the mornin', blues fallin' down like rain.

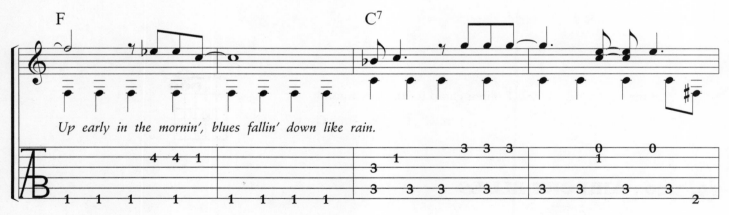

Up early in the mornin', blues fallin' down like rain.

Deep down in my heart, I felt an achin' pain.

#10 : EARLY MORNING BLUES (Key of C)

C7   F7   C7
Up early in the morning, blues fallin' down like rain.

F7   C7
Up early in the morning, blues fallin' down like rain.

G7   F7   C7 F7 C G7
Deep down in my heart I felt an achin' pain.

C7   F7   C7
Ain't it hard to wake up, wake up all by yourself.

F7   C7
Ain't it hard to wake up, wake up all by yourself.

            G7   F7   C7 F7 C G7
When the one you're lovin' has gone off with someone else.

C7   F7   C7
In the evening, can't you hear me when I call.

F7   C7
In the evening, can't you hear me when I call.

G7   F7   C7 F7 C G7
Late in the night time, that's when I miss you most of all.

BOOGIE BASS LINES

THAT'S ALRIGHT pattern

19

#11 : THAT'S ALRIGHT (Key of C)

C7   F7   C7

That's alright, that's alright with me.

F7   C7

That's alright, that's alright with me.

G7   F7   C7 F G G7

Anyway you want it, that's the way it's gonna be.

#11, 1:05 : THAT'S ALRIGHT

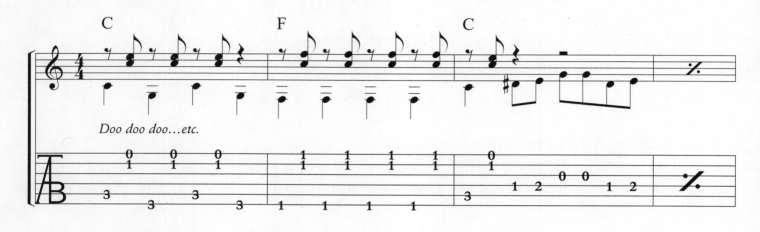

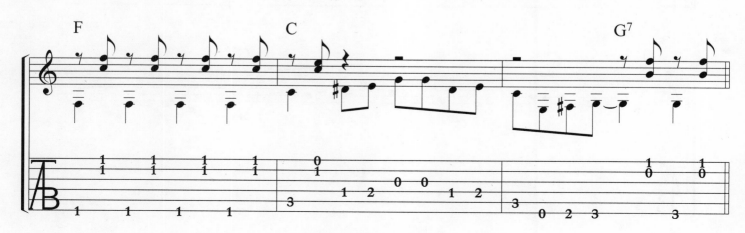

20

#11 : TWELVE BAR BLUES (Key of C)

C7   F7   C7
Twelve bar blues, twelve bar blues, twelve bar blues, twelve bar blues,

G7   F7   C C7 F Fm C G7
Twelve bar blues; you can play it all night and day.

C7   F7   C7
Same old thing, same old thing, same old thing, same old thing,

G7   F7   C C7 F Fm C G7
Same old thing, it sure sounds good to me.

#12, 1:35 : WORRIED BLUES

Got the worried blues,   I'm blue as I can be.

Worried blues, blue as I can be.   Said I

got more worries than the fishes in the deep blue sea.

#12 : WORRIED BLUES

C   C7
I got the worried blues, blue as I can be.

      F   C
Got the worried blues, blue as I can be.

 G7   F   C
I got more troubles than there's fishes in the deep blue sea.

     C   C7
Well, I want somebody to tell me what's wrong with me.

  F   C
I want somebody to tell me what's wrong with me.

    G7   C
These worried blues just won't let me be.

     C   C7
Got the worried blues, worried all the time.

    F   C
Got the worried blues, worried all the time.

G7   C
Just can't get these worries off my mind.

#13 : NEW CHORDS FOR THE KEY OF G :

D   D⁷   G⁷

  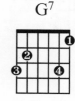

#13 : HESITATION BLUES (Key of G)

  G
I'm standin' on the corner with a dollar in my hand,

           G7
Lookin' for a woman who's lookin' for a man. Tell me

C   G   D7   G
How long must I wait ? Can I get you now, or must I hesitate ?

G
If the river was whiskey and I was a duck,

           G7
I'd swim to the bottom and never come up. Tell me…(etc.)

G
The eagle on a dollar says "In God we trust."

                G7
A woman says she wants a man but wants to see a dollar first. Tell me…(etc.)

#13, 2:40
TURNAROUND LICK

#14
VARIATIONS OF THE BASIC FINGERPICKING PATTERN

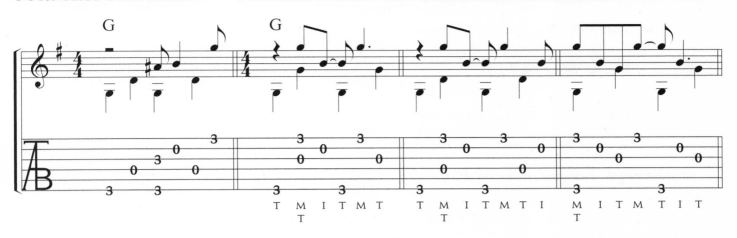

#15, 0:45 : WORRIED BLUES (Key of G)

Worried blues,   *worried all the time.*

Got the worried blues, Lord. I'm worried all the time.

Just can't get these troubles off my mind.

#15 : WORRIED BLUES (Key of G)

G   G7
Got the worried blues, blue as I can be.

C   G
Worried blues, blue as I can be.

D7   G
Got more troubles than fishes in the deep blue sea.

G   G7
Some people tell me worried blues ain't bad.

C   G
Some people say the worried blues ain't bad.

       D7   G
It must not have been the more worried blues they had.

G   G7
Worried blues, worried all the time.

C   G
Worried blues, worried all the time.

D7   G
Just can't get these troubles off my mind.

#15, 1:30 : "NICE LICKS"

#16 : BOOGIE BASS LINES (Key of G)

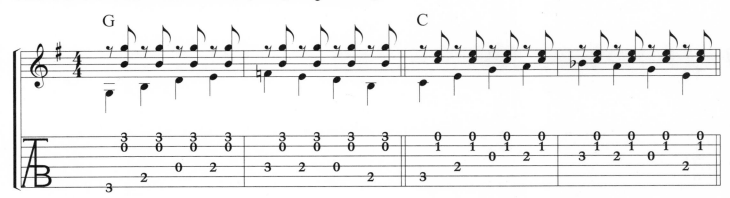

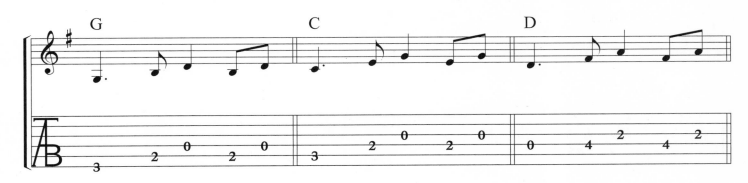

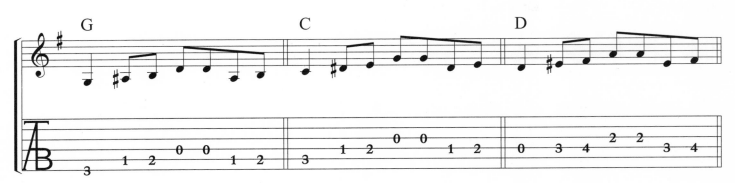

#18 : AIRPORT BLUES (KEY of G)

G   G7   C   C7
Take me to the airport, won't you put me on a plane,

  G7   D7   G G7 C G D7
This smoggy old city, it's drivin' me insane.

#17 : EARLY MORNING BLUES

18 : KEY of G TURNAROUND

#19 : I – IV – V CHORD FAMILIES

	I	IV	V
Key of E:	E	A	B7
Key of C:	C	F	G7
Key of G:	G	C	D7

#20 : TWELVE BAR BLUES (Key of G)

G7   C7   G7

Twelve bar blues, twelve bar blues, twelve bar blues, twelve bar blues,

D7   C7   G (turnaround)

Twelve bar blues, you can play it all night and day.

#21 : EARLY MORNING BLUES

#22 : NEW BASS RUNS FOR KEY of G

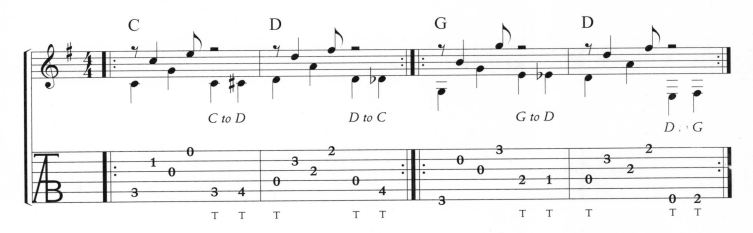

#24 : CALL ME A DOG

G   E7   A7
Well it's call me a dog when I'm gone, gone, gone,

D7   G
Call me a dog when I'm gone.

     E7   A7
But when you see me comin' with a twenty dollar bill,

     D7   G
It's "Honey, where you been so long ¿"

E7   A7
Where did you get that pretty red dress, and the

D7   G
Shoes you're wearing so fine ¿

   E7   A7
I got my dress from an engineer,

   D7   G
Shoes from a worker in the mine.

#24, 0:35 : CALL ME A DOG

And it's where did you get the pret - ty red dress, and the
Got my dress from an en - gin - eer, got my

shoes you're wear - in' so fine ?
shoes from a work - er in the mine.

I

#24, 1:45 : BANJO ROLLS

T T IM TIM TIM T TIMTIM T IM T

#24, 2:45 : TURNAROUND

T T T T T T

Eb7

30

CD #3 – Blues Soloing in E, C and G

#3 : THE E BLUES SCALE

← left hand fingering

#4, 2:14 : EARLY MORNING BLUES

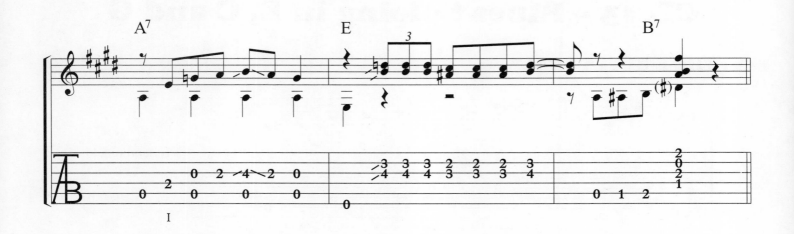

#5, 1:34 : AIRPORT BLUES

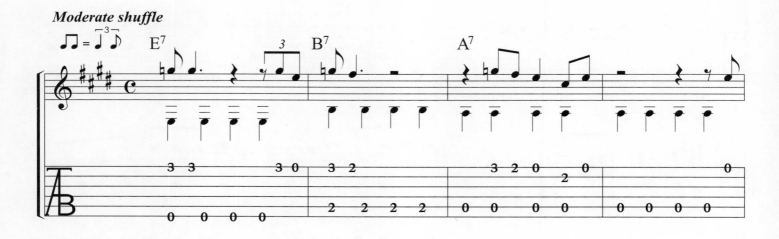

#6, 2:10 : THAT'S ALRIGHT

#7, 2:20 : TWELVE BAR BLUES

Bright shuffle

#8, 3:50 : WORRIED BLUES

#9 : G MAJOR SCALE

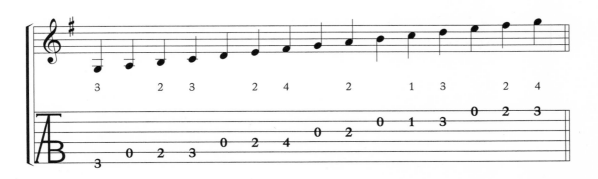

#10, 1:23 : HESITATION BLUES

#11, 1:02 : COCAINE

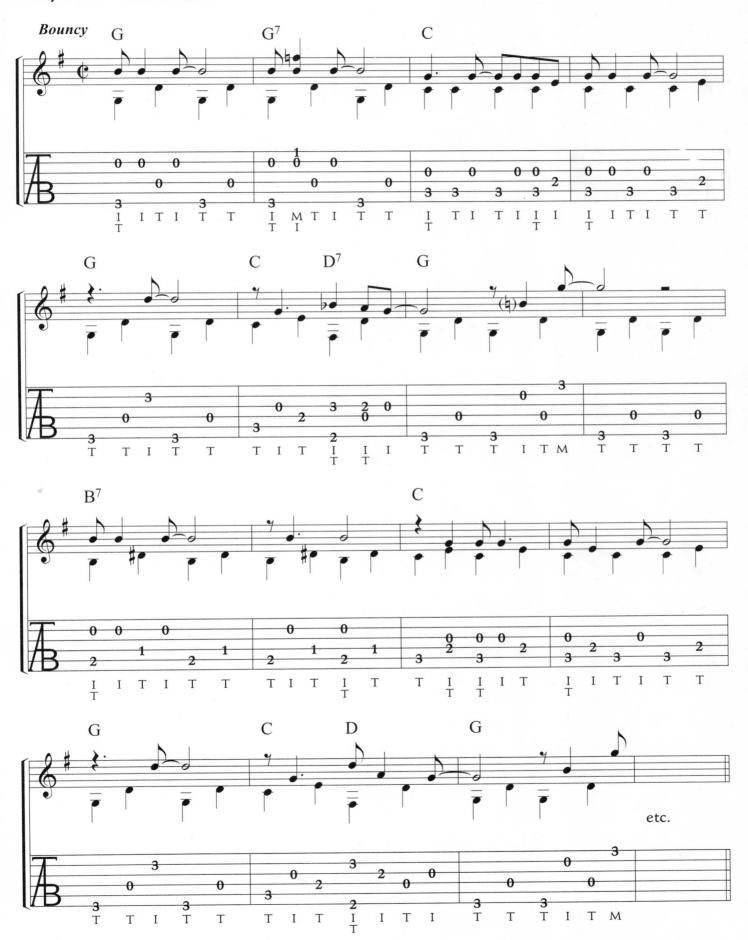

#12, 1:05 : WORRIED BLUES

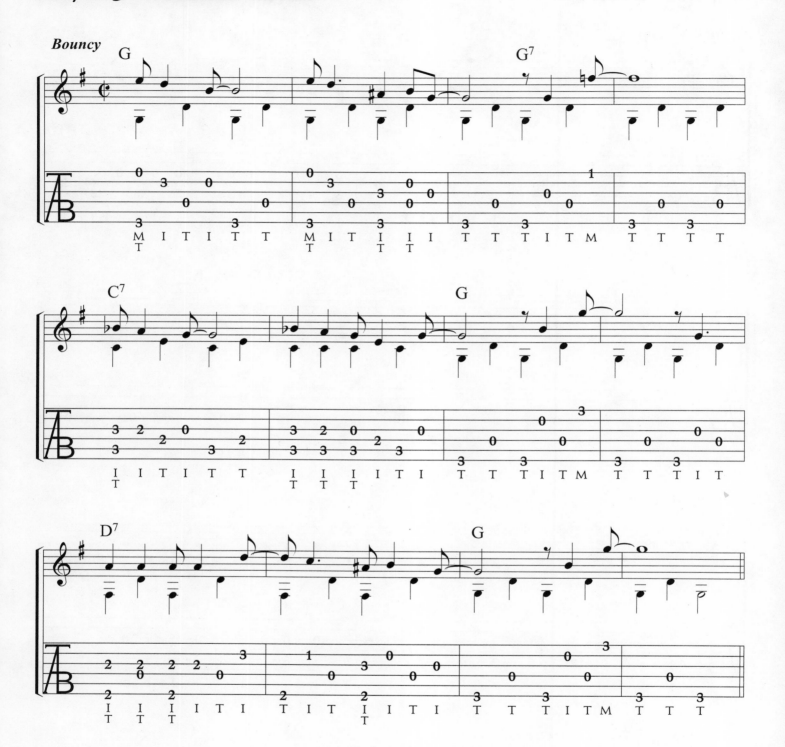

#13, 2:10 : EARLY MORNING BLUES

#14, 1:00 : AIRPORT BLUES

#15, 0:47 : THAT'S ALRIGHT

etc. (turnaround)

#16, 0:54 : TWELVE BAR BLUES

#16, 1:20 : C MAJOR SCALE

#17, 0:50 : COCAINE

#18, 0:55 : HESITATION BLUES

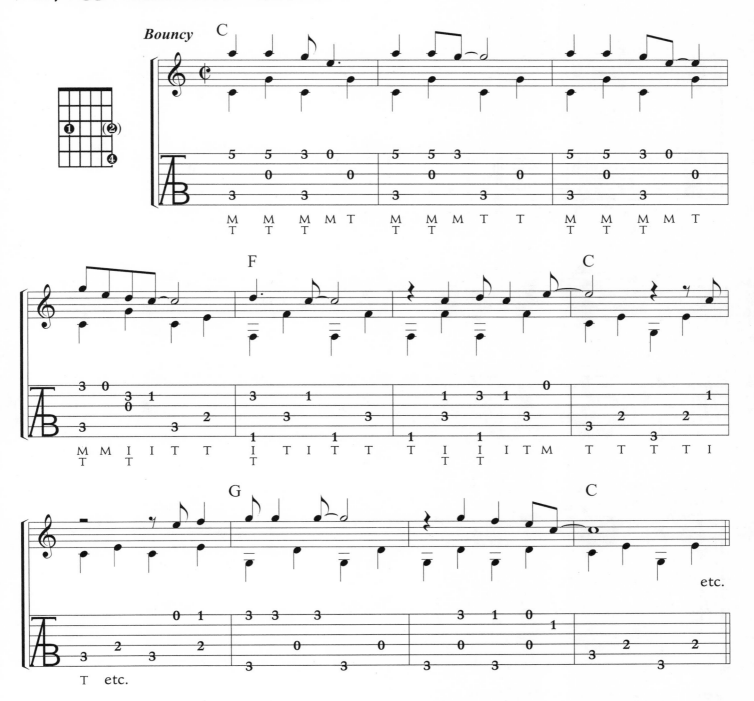

Alternate way to play the first few bars:

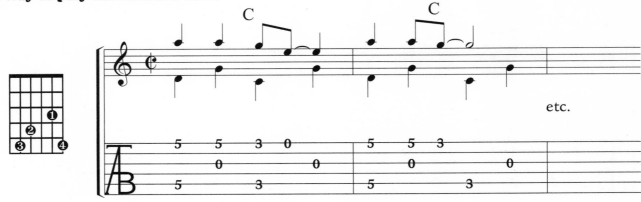

#19, 0:35 : WORRIED BLUES

#20 : EARLY MORNING BLUES

#21, 0:33 : AIRPORT BLUES

Moderate shuffle

#22, 0:37 : THAT'S ALRIGHT

46

#23, 0:43 : TWELVE BAR BLUES

Bright shuffle

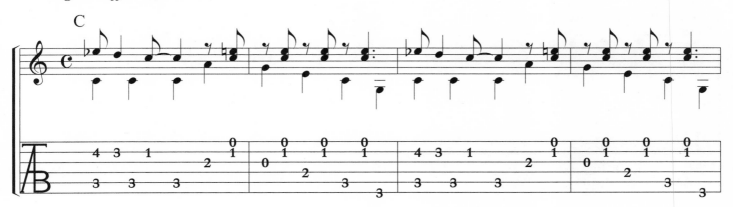

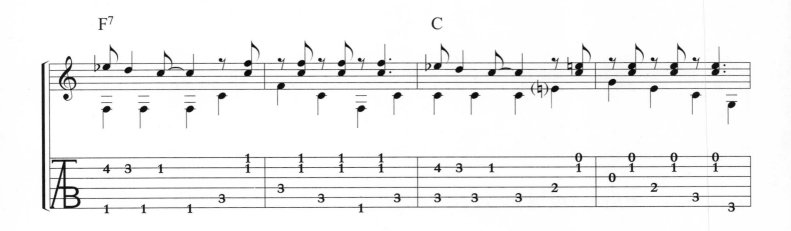

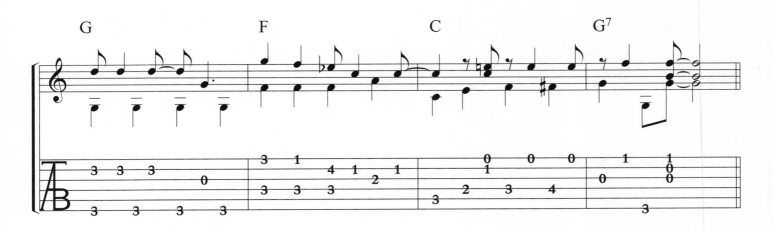

24, 0:42 : CALL ME A DOG (Key of C)

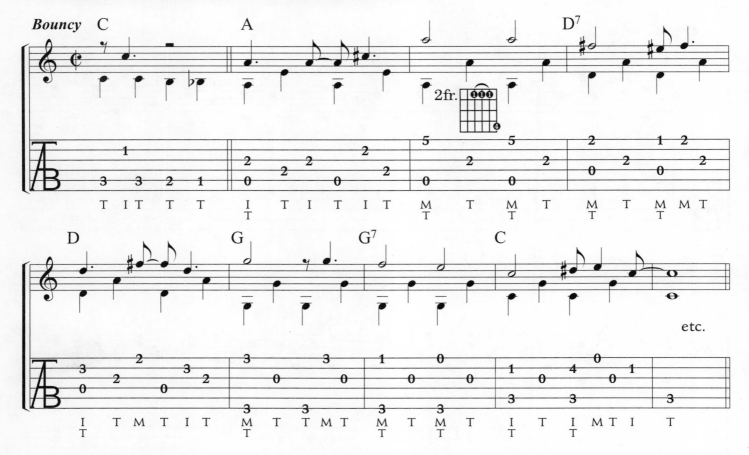

24, 1:18 : CALL ME A DOG (Key of G)

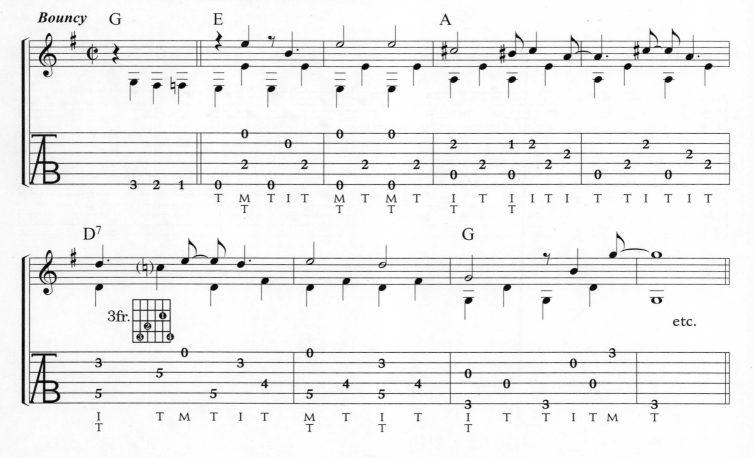